Are You My Wine?

Are You My Wine?

A Children's Book Parody Exploring the World of Wine

by **Reese Ling**
illustrated by **Angela Jazmine**

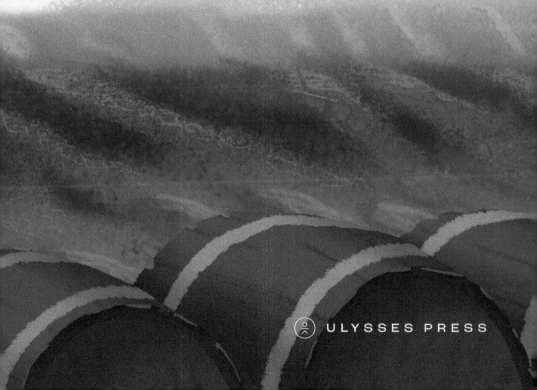

⊙ ULYSSES PRESS

Published in the United States by:
Ulysses Press
PO Box 3440
Berkeley, CA 94703
www.ulyssespress.com

ISBN: 978-1-61243-257-9
Library of Congress Catalog Number: 2016957524

Printed in the United States
10 9 8 7 6 5 4 3 2 1

Acquisitions: Casie Vogel
Managing Editor: Claire Chun
Editor: Shayna Keyles
Proofreader: Renee Rutledge

in vino veritas
—Pliny the Elder

Inside the office,

Penguin worked.
   He worked
      and worked
         and worked.

Until ... FINALLY ... it was 5 o'clock.

"Where should I go for a drink?" Penguin asked aloud.

There was a wine bar downtown where his friends hung out,
but Penguin did not know much about wine.

Penguin proclaimed, "Tonight's the night. I will go and look for *my* wine!" Out of the office he went. Down, down, down, until he heard a *pop!*

Penguin spotted his friend. "Good evening, Hummingbird."

"*Bonjour*, Penguin. Would you like to join me for a glass of Champagne?"

"Why yes, thank you. Is this French?" asked Penguin.

"But of course," replied Hummingbird. "Sparkling wines come from many places, but only those from France's Champagne region are called Champagne."

Penguin looked at the wine and smelled its aroma. He let a small amount of the Champagne roll around in his mouth before swallowing. "It's very refreshing, and the bubbles are fun! Could this be my wine?"

"*Pourquoi pas?* It's a less fruity, more acidic wine that's perfect for any celebration," explained Hummingbird.

"Thank you again," Penguin said while emptying his flute and excusing himself. "I'll go inside now and try some other wines."

"*Au revoir!*" trilled Hummingbird with a friendly flutter.

Inside the bar Penguin approached his friend Mouse, who was drinking a light white wine. "Greetings, Mouse, mind if I join you?"

"Not at all," squeaked Mouse.

"I'm here tonight to look for my wine," said Penguin.

"Then you must try some of my Pinot Grigio," insisted Mouse as he poured Penguin a glass.

Penguin detected a floral fragrance, almost like honeysuckle. He took a sip. "It tastes like citrus!" he said, sounding surprised.

"Yeah!" laughed Mouse. "Pinot Grigio often tastes like limes, lemons, pears, nectarines, or apples. Which is why it is a perfect match for my Brie, Gouda, and cheddar cheese plate!"

"I'm not a big cheese eater like you, Mouse," Penguin teased, "but this is a delightful wine simply by itself."

After thanking Mouse for the wine, Penguin ambled over to Bunny. "Hello, Bunny."

"Hello, Penguin."

"Is that Pinot Grigio as well?" asked Penguin.

"No," Bunny responded. "It's Sauvignon Blanc, an herbal, grassy wine that's super fruity and completely dry. It has flavors that range from peach, melon, and grapefruit, all the way to bell pepper, jalapeño, and—my favorite—grass."

"Maybe this is my wine?" Penguin pondered aloud.

"Here, try a glass," Bunny offered. "I think you will like it. It's one of the most popular wines. In fact, Sauvignon Blanc is one of the most widely planted grapes in the world."

"I can see why people like it," admitted Penguin after finishing the pour. And yet he wondered. Just because it's popular, does that mean it is my wine? He decided to try some more.

Nearby, the Koala twins were also enjoying some white wine. "Hi, Koalas, am I interrupting?"

"Not at all, come join us!" The twins replied in unison.

"I'm curious about the wines you are drinking," Penguin said a bit too loudly. "Maybe one of them is my wine."

"You're welcome to have some of mine," offered Koala while adjusting his bow tie. "It's a Chardonnay that's rich and creamy, like butter."

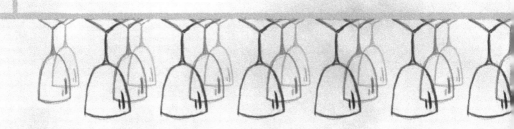

"Mmm, Chardonnay is delicious." And without missing a beat, Penguin turned and asked, "Can I try your wine?" The other twin happily handed over his glass and Penguin took a sip.

"Oh, how different," gushed Penguin. "It's light and fruity. It makes me think of pineapples … of the tropics … like the flowers on your shirt. What is this delightful wine?"

"It's Chardonnay, too!"

"Huh? How can they be so different?" asked a confused Penguin.

"Chardonnay, like most wine, changes depending on how it's made and where it's grown. Creamy or zesty, it's still a Chardonnay."

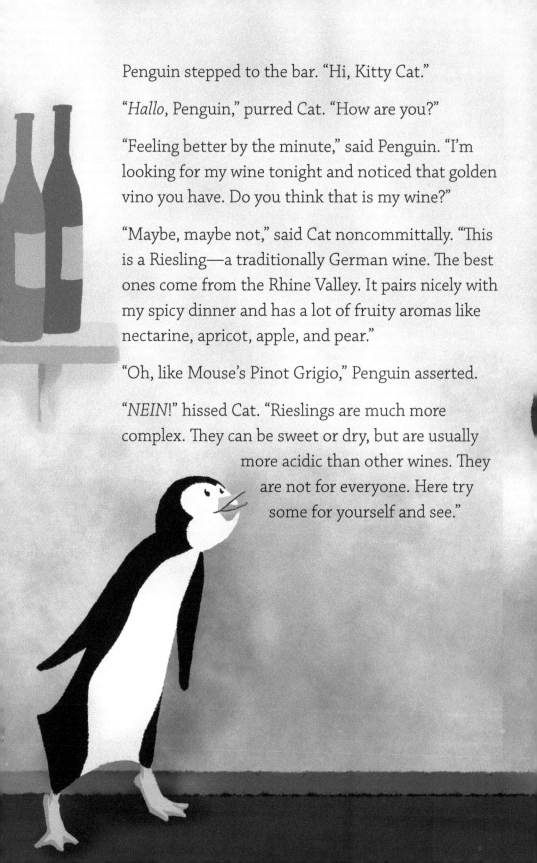

Penguin stepped to the bar. "Hi, Kitty Cat."

"*Hallo*, Penguin," purred Cat. "How are you?"

"Feeling better by the minute," said Penguin. "I'm looking for my wine tonight and noticed that golden vino you have. Do you think that is my wine?"

"Maybe, maybe not," said Cat noncommittally. "This is a Riesling—a traditionally German wine. The best ones come from the Rhine Valley. It pairs nicely with my spicy dinner and has a lot of fruity aromas like nectarine, apricot, apple, and pear."

"Oh, like Mouse's Pinot Grigio," Penguin asserted.

"*NEIN!*" hissed Cat. "Rieslings are much more complex. They can be sweet or dry, but are usually more acidic than other wines. They are not for everyone. Here try some for yourself and see."

Penguin sampled a glass. "This is a very interesting and curious wine, Cat. I'm not sure what to think of it just yet. Maybe I should try some other options to compare."

"Do as you wish," said Cat indifferently as he turned back to his dinner.

Penguin hopped onto the stool next to Flamingo. "Hey, Flamingo. You are looking stylish tonight."

"I always look stylish and you know it," she said, and the two friends shared a laugh.

"That's a pretty pink wine," said Penguin. "Is that my wine?"

Brunch

EGGS BENEDICT
PARISIAN OMELET
BELGIAN WAFFLES
BRIOCHE FRENCH TOAST

"I don't know. But I know it's *mine*," sassed Flamingo. "This is a Rosé. You must try a glass. It's sweet, but crisp and served chilled. It's a good wine for brunch although personally, I drink Rosé all day, every day."

Penguin took a hearty gulp. "Very fruity and refreshing. But why is it pink?"

"Wine gets its color from the grape skins. For red wines, the skins sit in the vat for a long time; but for Rosé, the skins are strained out sooner. There's a whole spectrum of rose colors, but for me, the pinker the better!" said Flamingo.

"I like it," admitted Penguin. "But now I'm curious to sample some darker red wines."

"Howdy, Monkey," howled Penguin as he approached his friend, who was holding a glass of light red wine.

"What's up?" smiled Monkey.

"What's that?" asked Penguin. "Is that my wine?"

"It's Pinot Noir, pal. You'll probably like it. It's a real crowd-pleaser. I serve it at all my parties. No one can turn away this wine."

"Why is it soooo popular, Monkey?"

"'Cause Pinot Noir is super versatile and grows all over the world! It goes well with everything from lighter foods like fish to richer meats like chicken and duck. Pinot Noir usually has cranberry, cherry, and raspberry notes, but can also mix in vanilla, licorice, tobacco, and even truffle flavors. Have a bit."

Penguin knocked back the rest of Monkey's wine. "Scrumptious!"

Monkey raised an eyebrow. "So, *was* that your wine?"

"I don't know, maybe. I want to find my *perfect* wine ... so I better keep looking." Penguin grinned.

Penguin tiptoed up behind Wolf and roused him with, "Hi ya, Wolfy."

Unfazed, Wolf glanced over his shoulder and greeted Penguin with a slick, toothy smile.

"That looks like a fine red wine you're enjoying," Penguin hinted. "Is that my wine?"

Getting his meaning, Wolf poured Penguin a glass. "Here you go, my little feathered friend. Try some Merlot. It's sleek and velvety with seductive flavors like chocolate, berries, and sometimes even espresso."

"Oh, that is really silky," Penguin agreed. "Does it go well with fish? You know how much I love fish."

"Oh no, not fish. It's great with a juicy, meaty dinner. Perfect for carnivores like me." Wolf said licking his lips. "Trust me, Merlot really is one of the best," he added with a sly wink.

Penguin replied, "Hmm, I can see why you like it, but, ummm, I think I'll go see what Hippo has over there," slowly edging to the far side of the table.

"Yo yo, Hippo," rhymed Penguin. "Are you also drinking Merlot?"

"No, I like something a little heavier," giggled Hippo. "I'm spicing up date night with a Zinfandel. Here, try it and see what you think."

"Wow, it tastes like berries!" Penguin exclaimed.

"Yes, strawberry, blackberry, even boysenberry flavors are common," Hippo elaborated. "That sweetness pairs well with spicier food, like barbecue or curry."

"Wait, now there is a lingering flavor that seems savory."

Hippo nodded. "Uh huh, that is called the 'finish.' It's the flavor that remains on your tongue even after you swallow. Zinfandel often has a bold, memorable finish, like licorice or tobacco."

"That's so cool. Wine is amazing. I need to try every one!" Penguin spouted exuberantly.

Penguin plopped down next to Panda. "What's up, Panda? What's that red wine? What's it like? Is that my wine? Can I have some?"

Amused by Penguin's gleeful entrance, Panda served him a heavy pour and expounded, "This is a full-bodied Cabernet Sauvignon. It's heavy, but not the heaviest. You can taste fruits like cherry and currant, but also some savory hints of black pepper and bell pepper."

"I see," said Penguin, taking a gulp.

"In fact, 100% Cabernet Sauvignon wines are very rare. You'll probably find them mixed with other varietals," continued Panda.

"Interesting," said Penguin, taking another gulp. "What is a varietal?"

"Varietals are the different types of grapes. Sometimes winemakers will mix varietals. Bordeaux blends are famous for combining the Cabernet Sauvignon and Merlot grapes."

"Who knew I was imbibing so many different grapes?" Penguin took the last swig from his glass and stood to leave. "And with that, I thank you, good sir. You are a gentleman ... and a scholar."

Penguin sidled over to Gorilla, who was devouring a rack of barbecued ribs. "Evening, 'rilla."

"Hi, Penguin. What brings you out tonight?"

"I'm looking for my wine and I saw you enjoying this dark red wine. Mind if I see what it's like?" Penguin said while simultaneously filling a glass from the open bottle on the table.

"Help yourself," Gorilla chuckled. "It's a Malbec, which usually comes from Argentina or France. This one from the Andean foothills has a bold fruity taste—lots of plum and raspberry with a little chocolate mixed in. French Malbecs tend to be spicier and can be more acidic."

"Oh yes, this *is* rich." Penguin guzzled the rest of the glass.

"You certainly enjoyed that quickly! Maybe you should switch to water for the rest of—"

"Oh wait!" Penguin interrupted. "What does Elephant have over there?"

Penguin stomped deliberately to Elephant's table, leaning on it to steady himself. "How do? Ellie-Ellie-Elephant."

"Good evening, Penguin."

"What are you slurpin'? I want some," blurted Penguin.

"Okay ... you can have a drink, but a *small* one. Don't worry. You don't need a lot to appreciate this wine. It's a big and luscious Syrah, the darkest of the red wines." Elephant handed Penguin her glass.

"It's delicious!" trumpeted Penguin.

"It sure is. And it goes perfectly with big, decadent, over-the-top meals and strong flavors. It is known as 'fruit forward' with flavors that range from sweet blueberry to savory black olive."

"Whoa, that soundsss intenssse," slurred Penguin.

"I always say, go big or go home! And Penguin, it sounds like you've gone big already, so maybe you should go home now."

"Not just yet," objected Penguin. "Look over there. Bear has a wine I haven't tried yet. What if Bear's wine is my wine?"

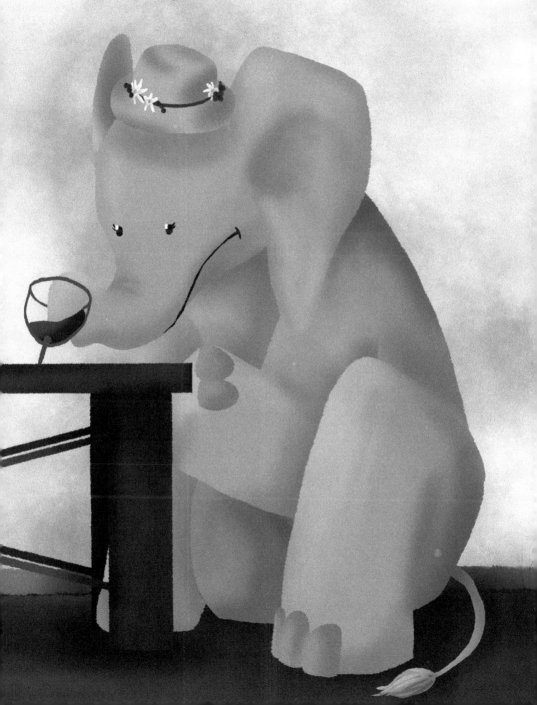

"BEAR!" shouted Penguin. "Give me a hug, big guy."

"Easy there, Penguin. I'm trying to savor my dessert."

"You sure are. Look at that tempting spread of treats. And you're having a glass of wine with them as well?"

"Yes, I'm capping off a fantastic evening with a dessert wine. This is Port, but there are other ones, including sherry and Madeira. They are all very sweet, almost syrupy like honey, and pair well with sugary treats," said Bear.

"Could Port be my wine?" said Penguin.

"Here, have a sip and see if it is."

"This *is* sweet," Penguin sighed contentedly. "And delightful. It's almost like a dessert itself!"

"Yes, it is a lovely end to a meal," agreed Bear.

"Thanks again, Bear. I wish I could share more wine with everyone but I've drunk my limit for tonight. It's time to hail a cab and head home." Penguin walked toward the exit.

"But, did you find your wine?"

"Yes, I know my wine.

"My wine is not Champagne, Pinot Grigio, Sauvignon Blanc, Chardonnay, or Riesling.

"My wine is not Rosé, Pinot Noir, Merlot, or Zinfandel.

"My wine is not Cabernet Sauvignon, Malbec, Syrah, or even Port."

"Then what wine is your wine?" called out Bear.

"All of them! *All* wines are my wine!" proclaimed Penguin.

About the Author

Reese Ling was born and aged in Napa Valley, California. She's traveled the wide world of wine, tasting grapes from Croatia to Australia. Her house is decorated with wine corks and punny signs, her favorites being "Rosé all day," "It's wine o'clock somewhere," and "Sip happens." This is her first book, inspired by her quest to make everyone a wino.

About the Illustrator

Angela Jazmine, a native of Maryland, has been telling stories visually for over five years as an animator in the video marketing industry. In addition to her award-winning work in animation, Angela has been an illustrator and designer for character development projects. She has a BFA from Savannah College of Art and Design, and in 2016 was honored as the Marketer of the Year by the American Advertising Federation of Greater Frederick.

For more information about Angela's work or to contact her, visit AngelaJazmine.com.